Step
Lightly

Step Lightly

Poems for the Journey

COLLECTED BY

Nancy Willard

Harcourt Brace & Company

San Diego   New York   London

Library of Congress Cataloging-in-Publication Data
Step lightly: poems for the journey/[edited by] Nancy Willard.
p.   cm.
Summary: A collection of poems celebrating the ordinary
in an unordinary way, by such authors as Emily Dickinson,
Theodore Roethke, and D. H. Lawrence.
ISBN 0-15-201849-2   ISBN 0-15-202052-7 pb
I. Young adult poetry, American.   2. Young adult poetry,
English.   [I. American poetry—Collections.   2. English
poetry—Collections.]   I. Willard, Nancy.
PS586.3.S74   1998
811.008'09283—dc21   98-5228

Text set in Centaur
Designed by Camilla Filancia
First edition
F E D C B A
Printed in the United States of America

For NANCY KRIM,

and all teachers who instill

in their students a passion for poetry

CONTENTS

Step
Lightly

INTRODUCTION

The book you are holding in your hands started in a shoe box. For years I've copied and clipped and saved poems from newspapers and magazines and books, because they gave me the special kind of pleasure that good poetry gives when it celebrates the ordinary in an unordinary way.

This is not an anthology of light verse. Though many of the poems have their own quirky humor, they also have the clarity of a well-lit room, and they move as gracefully and accurately as a cat stepping across a desk crowded with objects.

If you read straight through this book, you can start in the morning with Emily Dickinson's "Will there really be a 'Morning'?" In the afternoon you can explore a sunlit garden with Theodore Roethke and converse with William Blake's tiger, Gerald Stern's cows, or Christopher Smart's cat. By the end of the day I hope your head will be spinning with so many memories of your own that you'll need Denise Levertov's "Writing in the Dark" to help you put them on paper.

These poems are for anyone who loves the sound of words and the rhythm of language. They are rhymed and unrhymed, traditional and experimental. There is one poem made up of prose lines from a tropical fish magazine, rearranged to suggest how a catfish might see himself.

Some of the poets in this book are well known. Others are just starting out on the long journey of writing. To borrow a phrase from Philip Levine, they are burning the little candle of their breath and making light of it all.

Nancy Willard

Emily Dickinson
"WILL THERE REALLY BE A 'MORNING'?"

Will there really be a "Morning"?
Is there such a thing as "Day"?
Could I see it from the mountains
If I were as tall as they?

Has it feet like Water lilies?
Has it feathers like a Bird?
Is it brought from famous countries
Of which I have never heard?

Oh some Scholar! Oh some Sailor!
Oh some Wise Man from the skies!
Please to tell a little Pilgrim
Where the place called "Morning" lies!

Michael Dennis Browne

FOR CAITLIN LALLY
(born February 1968)

I heard a bird
　　　　From a gold tree sing:
This is the beginning
　　　　Of everything.

And then a worm
　　　　From the dark earth spoke:
This is the morning
　　　　That I awoke.

And so in your world,
　　　　O woman, O man;
Like the worm, I awoke,
　　　　Like the bird, I began.

D. H. Lawrence
THE WHITE HORSE

The youth walks up to the white horse, to put its halter on
and the horse looks at him in silence.
They are so silent they are in another world.

James Wright

MUTTERINGS OVER THE CRIB OF A DEAF CHILD

"How will he hear the bell at school
Arrange the broken afternoon,
And know to run across the cool
Grasses where the starlings cry,
Or understand the day is gone?"

Well, someone lifting curious brows
Will take the measure of the clock.
And he will see the birchen boughs
Outside sagging dark from the sky,
And the shade crawling upon the rock.

"And how will he know to rise at morning?
His mother has other sons to waken,
She has the stove she must build to burning
Before the coals of the nighttime die;
And he never stirs when he is shaken."

I take it the air affects the skin,
And you remember, when you were young,
Sometimes you could feel the dawn begin,
And the fire would call you, by and by,
Out of the bed and bring you along.

"Well, good enough. To serve his needs
All kinds of arrangements can be made.
But what will you do if his finger bleeds?
Or a bobwhite whistles invisibly
And flutes like an angel off in the shade?"

He will learn pain. And, as for the bird,
It is always darkening when that comes out.
I will putter as though I had not heard,
And lift him into my arms and sing
Whether he hears my song or not.

Galway Kinnell
From THE AVENUE BEARING THE INITIAL
OF CHRIST INTO THE NEW WORLD

I

pcheek pcheek pcheek pcheek pcheek
They cry. The motherbirds thieve the air
To appease them. A tug on the East River
Blasts the bass-note of its passage, lifted
From the infra-bass of the sea. A broom
Swishes over the sidewalk like feet through leaves.
Valerio's pushcart Ice Coal Kerosene
Moves clack
                        clack
                           clack
On a broken wheelrim. Ringing in its chains
The New Star Laundry horse comes down the street
Like a roofleak whucking into a pail.
At the redlight, where a horn blares,
The Golden Harvest Bakery brakes on its gears,
Squeaks, and seethes in place. A propane-
gassed bus makes its way with big, airy sighs.

Across the street a woman throws open
Her window,
She sets, terribly softly,
Two potted plants on the windowledge
                 tic   tic
And bangs shut her window.

A man leaves a doorway tic toc tic toc tic toc tic hurrah
            toc splat on Avenue C tic etc and turns the corner.
Banking the same corner
A pigeon coasts 5th Street in shadows,
Looks for altitude, surmounts the rims of buildings,
And turns white.

The babybirds pipe down. It is day.

Liz Fischer
TURNING THE TIDE

Oh the lovely
oh the love in
oh to be loved
I sweep the tide in.

Lick my way out
to the sea
I

rise up to the water's cusp,
I
dive down to the fluid
          dusk,
I strain out all the ships and shells,
I cry to make the sea a well.

The lovely sight
of sea foam white:
the bluest surge,
the darkest gorge—
I pile the water
          onto the shore.

The loveliest sight,
in dawn—out night,
the crater deep,
the water so steep.

I heap all the water onto the land
    so you can
        cha
          cha
            cha
from the center of the sand.

Etain Mary Clarke
"THE WIND OF THE MARIGOLD"

The wind of the marigold,
The flies of the American Bird,
The shamrocks of the stones,
The Lord of the Fieldmice,
The marigold's lavender,
The marigold of the shamrocks,
The mice of the round-a-gold.
The tractors of the storm
How the wind blows
The wolves howl,
While the moon moves
Along in the sky.
The wind blows people's hats off
And blows people's dresses up,
The Lord Mayor of the Dreams,
The mari-of-the-golds,
The Lord Mayor of the Golds.

Theodore Roethke
CHILD ON TOP OF A GREENHOUSE

The wind billowing out the seat of my britches,
My feet crackling splinters of glass and dried putty,
The half-grown chrysanthemums staring up like accusers,
Up through the streaked glass, flashing with sunlight,
A few white clouds all rushing eastward,
A line of elms plunging and tossing like horses,
And everyone, everyone pointing up and shouting!

Denise Levertov
COME INTO ANIMAL PRESENCE

Come into animal presence.
No man is so guileless as
the serpent. The lonely white
rabbit on the roof is a star
twitching its ears at the rain.
The llama intricately
folding its hind legs to be seated
not disdains but mildly
disregards human approval.
What joy when the insouciant
armadillo glances at us and doesn't
quicken his trotting
across the track into the palm brush.

What is this joy? That no animal
falters, but knows what it must do?
That the snake has no blemish,
that the rabbit inspects his strange surroundings
in white star-silence? The llama
rests in dignity, the armadillo
has some intention to pursue in the palm-forest.

Those who were sacred have remained so,
holiness does not dissolve, it is a presence
of bronze, only the sight that saw it
faltered and turned from it.
An old joy returns in holy presence.

William Blake
THE TYGER

Tyger! Tyger! burning bright
In the forests of the night,
What immortal hand or eye
Could frame thy fearful symmetry?

In what distant deeps or skies
Burnt the fire of thine eyes?
On what wings dare he aspire?
What the hand dare seize the fire?

And what shoulder, and what art,
Could twist the sinews of thy heart?
And when thy heart began to beat,
What dread hand? and what dread feet?

What the hammer? what the chain?
In what furnace was thy brain?
What the anvil? what dread grasp
Dare its deadly terrors clasp?

When the stars threw down their spears,
And water'd heaven with their tears,
Did he smile his work to see?
Did he who made the Lamb make thee?

Tyger! Tyger! burning bright
In the forests of the night,
What immortal hand or eye,
Dare frame thy fearful symmetry?

Theodore Roethke
S L U G

How I loved one like you when I was little!—
With his stripes of silver and his small house on his back,
Making a slow journey around the well-curb.
I longed to be like him, and was,
In my way, close cousin
To the dirt, my knees scrubbing
The gravel, my nose wetter than his.

When I slip, just slightly, in the dark,
I know it isn't a wet leaf,
But you, loose toe from the old life,
The cold slime come into being,
A fat, five-inch appendage
Creeping slowly over the wet grass,
Eating the heart out of my garden.

And you refuse to die decently!—
Flying upward through the knives of my lawnmower
Like pieces of smoked eel or raw oyster,
And I go faster in my rage to get done with it,
Until I'm scraping and scratching at you, on the doormat,
The small dead pieces sticking under an instep;
Or, poisoned, dragging a white skein of spittle over a
    path—

Beautiful, in its way, like quicksilver—
You shrink to something less,
A rain-drenched fly or spider.

I'm sure I've been a toad, one time or another.
With bats, weasels, worms—I rejoice in the kinship.
Even the caterpillar I can love, and the various vermin.
But as for you, most odious—
Would Blake call you holy?

Liz Fischer
COVER CATFISH

Year in
and year out
one group of
fishes that continues to
rank
right near

the top
in popularity

despite their
lack of glamor
status, and
the fact that
no
one
ever
calls them

jewels of the aquarium
or
princes of the underwater kingdom

is
those hardy
and peaceful
undemanding
but
fascinating
armored
catfishes,

the Corydoras species.

Christopher Smart
"FOR I WILL CONSIDER MY CAT JEOFFRY"

For I will consider my Cat Jeoffry.

For he is the servant of the Living God duly and daily
serving him.

For at the first glance of the glory of God in the East he
worships in his way.

For this is done by wreathing his body seven times round
with elegant quickness.

For then he leaps up to catch the musk, which is the
blessing of God upon his prayer.

For he rolls upon prank to work it in.

For having done duty and received blessing he begins to
consider himself.

For this he performs in ten degrees.

For first he looks upon his fore-paws to see if they are clean.

For secondly he kicks up behind to clear away there.

For thirdly he works it upon stretch with the fore-paws
extended.

For fourthly he sharpens his paws by wood.

For fifthly he washes himself.

For sixthly he rolls upon wash.

For seventhly he fleas himself, that he may not be
interrupted upon the beat.

For eighthly he rubs himself against a post.

For ninthly he looks up for his instructions.

For tenthly he goes in quest of food.

For having consider'd God and himself he will consider his
neighbour.

For if he meets another cat he will kiss her in kindness.

For when he takes his prey he plays with it to give it a chance.

For one mouse in seven escapes by his dallying.

For when his day's work is done his business more properly
begins.

For he keeps the Lord's watch in the night against the
adversary.

How he counteracts the powers of darkness by his
electrical skin and glaring eyes.

For he counteracts the Devil, who is death, by brisking
about the life.

For in his morning orisons he loves the sun and the sun
loves him.

For he is of the tribe of Tiger.

For the Cherub Cat is a term of the Angel Tiger.

For he has the subtlety and hissing of a serpent, which in
goodness he suppresses.

For he will not do destruction if he is well fed, neither will
he spit without provocation.

For he purrs in thankfulness, when God tells him he's a
good Cat.

For he is an instrument for the children to learn
benevolence upon.

For every house is incomplete without him and a blessing
is lacking in the spirit.

Gerald Stern
COW WORSHIP

I love the cows best when they are a few feet away
from my dining-room window and my pine floor,
when they reach in to kiss me with their wet
mouths and their white noses.
I love them when they walk over the garbage cans
and across the cellar doors,
over the sidewalk and through the metal chairs
and the birdseed.
—Let me reach out through the thin curtains
and feel the warm air of May.
It is the temperature of the whole galaxy,
all the bright clouds and clusters,
beasts and heroes,
glittering singers and isolated thinkers
at pasture.

Federico García Lorca
THE LITTLE MUTE BOY

The little boy was looking for his voice.
(The king of the crickets had it.)
In a drop of water
the little boy was looking for his voice.

I do not want it for speaking with;
I will make a ring of it
so that he may wear my silence
on his little finger.

In a drop of water
the little boy was looking for his voice.

(The captive voice, far away,
put on a cricket's clothes.)

(Translated by W. S. Merwin)

Maxine Kumin

CREDO

I believe in magic. I believe in the rights
of animals to leap out of our skins
as recorded in the Kiowa legend:
Directly there was a bear where the boy had been

as I believe in the resurrected wake-robin,
first wet knob of trillium to knock
in April at the underside of earth's door
in central New Hampshire where bears are

though still denned up at that early greening.
I believe in living on grateful terms
with the earth, with the black crumbles
of ancient manure that sift through my fingers

when I topdress the garden for winter. I believe
in the wet strings of earthworms aroused out of season
and in the bear, asleep now in the rock cave
where my outermost pasture abuts the forest.

I cede him a swale of chokecherries in August.
I give the sow and her cub as much yardage
as they desire when our paths intersect
as does my horse shifting under me

respectful but not cowed by our encounter.
I believe in the gift of the horse, which is magic,
their deep fear-snorts in play when the wind comes up,
the ballet of nip and jostle, plunge and crow hop.

I trust them to run from me, necks arched in a full
swan's S, tails cocked up over their backs
like plumes on a Cavalier's hat. I trust them
to gallop back, skid to a stop, their nostrils

level with my mouth, asking for my human breath
that they may test its intent, taste the smell of it.
I believe in myself as their sanctuary
and the earth with its summer plumes of carrots,

its clamber of peas, beans, masses of tendrils
as mine. I believe in the acrobatics of boy
into bear, the grace of animals
in my keeping, the thrust to go on.

William Butler Yeats
THE SONG OF WANDERING AENGUS

I went out to the hazel wood,
Because a fire was in my head,
And cut and peeled a hazel wand,
And hooked a berry to a thread;
And when white moths were on the wing,
and moth-like stars were flickering out,
I dropped the berry in a stream
And caught a little silver trout.

When I had laid it on the floor
I went to blow the fire aflame,
But something rustled on the floor,
And some one called me by my name:
It had become a glimmering girl
With apple blossom in her hair
Who called me by my name and ran
And faded through the brightening air.

Though I am old with wandering
Through hollow lands and hilly lands,
I will find out where she has gone,
And kiss her lips and take her hands;

And walk among long dappled grass,
And pluck till time and times are done
The silver apples of the moon,
The golden apples of the sun.

Gabriela Mistral
LA MANCA (THE LITTLE GIRL THAT LOST A FINGER)

And a clam caught my little finger,
and the clam fell into the sand,
and the sand was swallowed by the sea,
and the whaler caught it in the sea,
and the whaler arrived at Gibraltar,
and in Gibraltar the fishermen sing:
'News of the earth we drag up from the sea,
news of a little girl's finger:
let her who lost it come get it!'

Give me a boat to go fetch it,
and for the boat give me a captain,
for the captain give me wages,
and for his wages let him ask for the city:
Marseilles with towers and squares and boats,
in all the wide world the finest city,
which won't be lovely with a little girl
that the sea robbed of her finger,
and that whalers chant for like town criers,
and that they're waiting for on Gibraltar . . .

(Translated by Muna Lee)

Robert Frost
THE WITCH OF COÖS

I stayed the night for shelter at a farm
Behind the mountain, with a mother and son,
Two old-believers. They did all the talking.

MOTHER.   Folks think a witch who has familiar spirits
She could call up to pass a winter evening,
But won't, should be burned at the stake or something.
Summoning spirits isn't "Button, button,
Who's got the button," I would have them know.

SON.   Mother can make a common table rear
And kick with two legs like an army mule.

MOTHER.   And when I've done it, what good have I done?
Rather than tip a table for you, let me
Tell you what Ralle the Sioux Control once told me.
He said the dead had souls, but when I asked him
How could that be—I thought the dead were souls—
He broke my trance. Don't that make you suspicious
That there's something the dead are keeping back?
Yes, there's something the dead are keeping back.

SON.   You wouldn't want to tell him what we have
Up attic, mother?

MOTHER.   Bones—a skeleton.

SON. But the headboard of mother's bed is pushed
Against the attic door: the door is nailed.
It's harmless. Mother hears it in the night,
Halting perplexed behind the barrier
Of door and headboard. Where it wants to get
Is back into the cellar where it came from.

MOTHER. We'll never let them, will we, son? We'll never!

SON. It left the cellar forty years ago
And carried itself like a pile of dishes
Up one flight from the cellar to the kitchen,
Another from the kitchen to the bedroom,
Another from the bedroom to the attic,
Right past both father and mother, and neither stopped it.
Father had gone upstairs; mother was downstairs.
I was a baby: I don't know where I was.

MOTHER. The only fault my husband found with me—
I went to sleep before I went to bed,
Especially in winter when the bed
Might just as well be ice and the clothes snow.
The night the bones came up the cellar stairs
Toffile had gone to bed alone and left me,
But left an open door to cool the room off
So as to sort of turn me out of it.
I was just coming to myself enough
To wonder where the cold was coming from,
When I heard Toffile upstairs in the bedroom

And thought I heard him downstairs in the cellar.
The board we had laid down to walk dry-shod on
When there was water in the cellar in spring
Struck the hard cellar bottom. And then someone
Began the stairs, two footsteps for each step,
The way a man with one leg and a crutch,
Or a little child, comes up. It wasn't Toffile:
It wasn't anyone who could be there.
The bulkhead double doors were double-locked
And swollen tight and buried under snow.
The cellar windows were banked up with sawdust
And swollen tight and buried under snow.
It was the bones. I knew them—and good reason.
My first impulse was to get to the knob
And hold the door. But the bones didn't try
The door; they halted helpless on the landing,
Waiting for things to happen in their favor.
The faintest restless rustling ran all through them.
I never could have done the thing I did
If the wish hadn't been too strong in me
To see how they were mounted for this walk.
I had a vision of them put together
Not like a man, but like a chandelier.
So suddenly I flung the door wide on him.
A moment he stood balancing with emotion,
And all but lost himself. (A tongue of fire
Flashed out and licked along his upper teeth.
Smoke rolled inside the sockets of his eyes.)

Then he came at me with one hand outstretched,
The way he did in life once; but this time
I struck the hand off brittle on the floor,
And fell back from him on the floor myself.
The finger-pieces slid in all directions.
(Where did I see one of those pieces lately?
Hand me my button box—it must be there.)
I sat up on the floor and shouted, "Toffile,
It's coming up to you." It had its choice
Of the door to the cellar or the hall.
It took the hall door for the novelty,
And set off briskly for so slow a thing,
Still going every which way in the joints, though,
So that it looked like lightning or a scribble,
From the slap I had just now given its hand.
I listened till it almost climbed the stairs
From the hall to the only finished bedroom,
Before I got up to do anything;
Then ran and shouted, "Shut the bedroom door,
Toffile, for my sake!" "Company?" he said,
"Don't make me get up; I'm too warm in bed."
So lying forward weakly on the handrail
I pushed myself upstairs, and in the light
(The kitchen had been dark) I had to own
I could see nothing. "Toffile, I don't see it.
It's with us in the room, though. It's the bones."
"What bones?" "The cellar bones—out of the grave."
That made him throw his bare legs out of bed

And sit up by me and take hold of me.
I wanted to put out the light and see
If I could see it, or else mow the room,
With our arms at the level of our knees,
And bring the chalk-pile down. "I'll tell you what—
It's looking for another door to try.
The uncommonly deep snow has made him think
Of his old song, 'The Wild Colonial Boy,'
He always used to sing along the tote road.
He's after an open door to get outdoors.
Let's trap him with an open door up attic."
Toffile agreed to that, and sure enough,
Almost the moment he was given an opening,
The steps began to climb the attic stairs.
I heard them. Toffile didn't seem to hear them.
"Quick!" I slammed to the door and held the knob.
"Toffile, get nails." I made him nail the door shut
And push the headboard of the bed against it.
Then we asked was there anything
Up attic that we'd ever want again.
The attic was less to us than the cellar.
If the bones liked the attic, let them have it.
Let them stay in the attic. When they sometimes
Come down the stairs at night and stand perplexed
Behind the door and headboard of the bed,
Brushing their chalky skull with chalky fingers,
With sounds like the dry rattling of a shutter,
That's what I sit up in the dark to say—

To no one anymore since Toffile died.
Let them stay in the attic since they went there.
I promised Toffile to be cruel to them
For helping them be cruel once to him.

SON.   We think they had a grave down in the cellar.

MOTHER.   We know they had a grave down in the cellar.

SON.   We never could find out whose bones they were.

MOTHER.   Yes, we could too, son. Tell the truth for once.
They were a man's his father killed for me.
I mean a man he killed instead of me.
The least I could do was help dig their grave.
We were about it one night in the cellar.
Son knows the story: but 'twas not for him
To tell the truth, suppose the time had come.
Son looks surprised to see me end a lie
We'd kept up all these years between ourselves
So as to have it ready for outsiders.
But tonight I don't care enough to lie—
I don't remember why I ever cared.
Toffile, if he were here, I don't believe
Could tell you why he ever cared himself. . . .

She hadn't found the finger-bone she wanted
Among the buttons poured out in her lap.
I verified the name next morning: Toffile.
The rural letter box said Toffile Lajway.

William Carlos Williams
SMELL!

Oh strong-ridged and deeply hollowed
nose of mine! what will you not be smelling?
What tactless asses we are, you and I boney nose
always indiscriminate, always unashamed,
and now it is the souring flowers of the bedraggled
poplars: a festering pulp on the wet earth
beneath them. With what deep thirst
we quicken our desires
to that rank odor of a passing springtime!
Can you not be decent? Can you not reserve your ardors
for something less unlovely? What girl will care
for us, do you think, if we continue in these ways?
Must you taste everything? Must you know everything?
Must you have a part in everything?

Elizabeth Bishop

MANNERS

For a child of 1918

My grandfather said to me
as we sat on the wagon seat,
"Be sure to remember to always
speak to everyone you meet."

We met a stranger on foot.
My grandfather's whip tapped his hat.
"Good day, sir. Good day. A fine day."
And I said it and bowed where I sat.

Then we overtook a boy we knew
with his big pet crow on his shoulder.
"Always offer everyone a ride;
don't forget that when you get older,"

my grandfather said. So Willy
climbed up with us, but the crow
gave a "Caw!" and flew off. I was worried.
How would he know where to go?

But he flew a little way at a time
from fence post to fence post, ahead;
and when Willy whistled he answered.
"A fine bird," my grandfather said,

"and he's well brought up. See, he answers
nicely when he's spoken to.
Man or beast, that's good manners.
Be sure that you both always do."

When automobiles went by,
the dust hid the people faces,
but we shouted "Good day! Good day!
Fine day!" at the top of our voices.

When we came to Hustler Hill,
he said that the mare was tired,
so we all got down and walked,
as our good manners required.

Kenneth Patchen
DAY OF RABBLEMENT

O come here! a sunflower!
No no no no
O hurry! hurry!
A sunflower is standing here!

No no no no

O come here!
There's a sunflower beside the wall!
No no no no
Great God! hurry! a sunflower!

No no no no

A sunflower!
Come! look at the sunflower!
Sunflower!
No no no no
Then tell me why you
Won't come!
No no no no

No no no no

Emily Hahn
WIND BLOWING

Wind blowing, wind blowing, looking for a fight,
Looking for a barrier all through the night,
Nothing left to blow against, nothing left to bite!

I can see everything, all round the earth;
Red sun dying, gold sun's birth;
Wind blowing frantically, scouring the earth.

Nothing, nothing anywhere, day and night and day:
Wind blew everywhere, blew it all away.

Nothing, nothing anywhere, night and day and night,
Poor wind blowing, looking for a fight,
Nothing left to blow against, nothing left to bite!

William Stafford
SANTA'S WORKSHOP

The doll bodies glide past on little
wires that glide through their eyes.
They never meet—the boys and girls
turn a corner side by side and
enter a distant room to be boxed
separately. One at a time they are
released from the wires. Their eyes
rest. With folded arms they
take their place, lie down,
go out to save the world.

Pablo Neruda
ODE TO A PAIR OF SOCKS

Maru Mori brought me
a pair
of socks
knitted with her shepherdess
hands,
two socks soft
as hares.
I slipped my feet
into them
as into
two
cases
knitted
with strands of
sunset
and the pelt of ewes.

Outrageous socks,
my feet were
two woolen
fish,
two large sharks,
of ultramarine blue

traversed
by a golden tress;
two gigantic blackbirds,
two cannon:
my feet
were honored
in this way
by these
celestial
socks.

So beautiful
were they
that for the first time
my feet seemed as unacceptable
as two decrepit firemen, firemen
unworthy
of that embroidered
fire,
of those luminous
socks.

Nevertheless,
I resisted
the acute temptation
to save them,
as college boys

collect
fireflies,
as the erudite
collect
sacred documents;
I resisted
the wild impulse
to place them
in a golden
cage
and each day feed them
birdseed
and rosy melon pulp.
Like the explorer
who in the jungle
surrenders the unique
fresh venison
to the roasting spit
and eats it
remorsefully,
I stretched out my feet
and encased them
in the
beautiful
socks,
and
then in my shoes.

And the moral of my ode
is this:
twice is beauty
beauty
and what is good is doubly
good
when it concerns two woolen
socks
in winter.

(Translated by Carlos Lozano)

Kelly Williams
THE BLUEST TATTOO

Anytime he asks me, "What's wrong with you?"
Anytime he asks me, "Baby, you got the blues?"
I hitch up my skirt, I unstrap my shoe—
I show him the blues—show him the bluest tattoo.

Oh, I carry my blues as a mark on my skin—
The blues are my body—just space to fill in.
It's a creature of sun, of air and of wind—
but most folks forget the cocoon it lived in.

My butterfly's got the ink—deep, thick blue—
My butterfly's gettin' lonely, been dreamin' of you.
Me, I'm lookin' down at it—such a cockeyed view—
Me, I'm thinkin' "Fly, baby!" and "What about gettin' two?"

Lucille Clifton
HOMAGE TO MY HIPS

these hips are big hips
they need space to
move around in.
they don't fit into little
petty places. these hips
are free hips.
they don't like to be held back.
these hips have never been enslaved,
they go where they want to go
they do what they want to do.
these hips are mighty hips.
these hips are magic hips.
i have known them
to put a spell on a man
and spin him like a top!

Nikki Giovanni
E G O - T R I P P I N G
(there may be a reason why)

I was born in the congo
I walked to the fertile crescent and built
        the sphinx
I designed a pyramid so tough that a star
        that only glows every one hundred years falls
        into the center giving divine perfect light
I am bad

I sat on the throne
        drinking nectar with allah
I got hot and sent an ice age to europe
        to cool my thirst
My oldest daughter is nefertiti
        the tears from my birth pains
        created the nile
I am a beautiful woman

I gazed on the forest and burned
        out the sahara desert
        with a packet of goat's meat
        and a change of clothes

I crossed it in two hours
I am a gazelle so swift
    so swift you can't catch me

    For a birthday present when he was three
I gave my son hannibal an elephant
    he gave me rome for mother's day
My strength flows ever on

My son noah built new/ark and
I stood proudly at the helm
    as we sailed on a soft summer day
I turned myself into myself and was
    jesus
    men intone my loving name

    All praises All praises
I am the one who would save

I sowed diamonds in my back yard
My bowels deliver uranium
    the filings from my fingernails are
    semi-precious jewels
    On a trip north
I caught a cold and blew
My nose giving oil to the arab world
I am so hip even my errors are correct

I sailed west to reach east and had to round off
      the earth as I went
      The hair from my head thinned and gold was laid
      across three continents
I am so perfect so divine so ethereal so surreal
I cannot be comprehended
      except by my permission

I mean . . . I . . . can fly
      like a bird in the sky . . .

William Carlos Williams
THE DESCENT OF WINTER (12/15)

What an image in the face of Almighty God is she
her hands in her slicker pockets, head bowed,
Tam pulled down, flat-backed, lanky-legged,
loose feet kicking the pebbles as she goes

Lucille Clifton
MISS ROSIE

when i watch you
wrapped up like garbage
sitting, surrounded by the smell
of too old potato peels
or
when i watch you
in your old man's shoes
with the little toe cut out
sitting, waiting for your mind
like next week's grocery
i say
when i watch you
you wet brown bag of a woman
who used to be the best looking gal in georgia
used to be called the Georgia Rose
i stand up
through your destruction
i stand up

Alexis Rotella
PURPLE

In first grade Mrs. Lohr
said my purple teepee
wasn't realistic enough,
that purple was no color
for a tent,
that purple was a color
for people who died,
that my drawing wasn't
good enough
to hang with the others.
I walked back to my seat
counting the swish swish swishes
of my baggy corduroy trousers.
With a black crayon
nightfall came
to my purple tent
in the middle
of an afternoon.

In second grade Mr. Barta
said draw anything;
he didn't care what.
I left my paper blank
and when he came around

to my desk
my heart beat like a tom tom.
He touched my head
with his big hand
and in a soft voice said
the snowfall
how clean
and white
and beautiful

Elizabeth Bishop
SESTINA

September rain falls on the house.
In the failing light, the old grandmother
sits in the kitchen with the child
beside the Little Marvel Stove,
reading the jokes from the almanac,
laughing and talking to hide her tears.

She thinks that her equinoctial tears
and the rain that beats on the roof of the house
were both foretold by the almanac,
but only known to a grandmother.
The iron kettle sings on the stove.
She cuts some bread and says to the child,

It's time for tea now; but the child
is watching the teakettle's small hard tears
dance like mad on the hot black stove,
the way the rain must dance on the house.
Tidying up, the old grandmother
hangs up the clever almanac

on its string. Birdlike, the almanac
hovers half open above the child,
hovers above the old grandmother

and her teacup full of dark brown tears.
She shivers and says she thinks the house
feels chilly, and puts more wood in the stove.

It was to be, says the Marvel Stove.
I know what I know, says the almanac.
With crayons the child draws a rigid house
and a winding pathway. Then the child
puts in a man with buttons like tears
and shows it proudly to the grandmother.

But secretly, while the grandmother
busies herself about the stove,
the little moons fall down like tears
from between the pages of the almanac
into the flower bed the child
has carefully placed in the front of the house.

Time to plant tears, says the almanac.
The grandmother sings to the marvelous stove
and the child draws another inscrutable house.

William Stafford
F A M E

My book fell in a river and rolled
over and over turning its pages
for the sun. From a bridge I saw this.
An eagle dived and snatched the slippery volume.

Now somewhere in the forest that book, educating
eagles, turns its leaves in the wind,
and all those poems whisper for autumn
to come, and the long nights, and the snow.

Radcliffe Squires
SNOW

Late snows spun from May rain come
Down heavy, wrecking tulips, breaking fruit
Trees. A gray sun stares at the fallen kindling wood.
But early snows, slanting in on autumn, shear
The trees of their burning fleece and, lying in
    the stubble, calm
It to pools of sulphur where sunlight comes to dream
Of the holy book it read on its long journey here.

Linda Pastan
BLIZZARD

the snow
has forgotten
how to stop
it falls
stuttering
at the glass
a silk windsock
of snow
blowing
under the porch light
tangling trees
which bend
like old women
snarled
in their own
knitting
snow drifts
up to the step
over the doorsill
a pointillist's blur
the wedding
of form and motion
shaping itself
to the wish of

any object it touches
chairs become
laps of snow
the moon could be
breaking apart
and falling
over the eaves
over the roof
a white bear
shaking its paw
at the window
splitting the hive
of winter
snow stinging
the air
I pull a comforter
of snow
up to my chin
and tumble
to sleep
as the whole
alphabet
of silence
falls out of the
sky

William Shakespeare
FULL FATHOM FIVE

"Full fathom five thy father lies,
      Of his bones are coral made:
Those are pearls that were his eyes.
      Nothing of him that doth fade,
But doth suffer a sea-change
Into something rich and strange . . .
Sea-nymphs hourly ring his knell."
                "Ding-dong."
"Hark! Now I hear them—Ding-dong, bell."

Donald Hall
NAMES OF HORSES

All winter your brute shoulders strained against collars,
    padding
and steerhide over the ash hames, to haul
sledges of cordwood for drying through spring and
    summer,
for the Glenwood stove next winter, and for the simmering
    range.

In April you pulled cartloads of manure to spread on the
    fields,
dark manure of Holsteins, and knobs of your own
    clustered with oats.
All summer you mowed the grass in meadow and hayfield,
    the mowing machine
clacketing beside you, while the sun walked high in the
    morning;

and after noon's heat, you pulled a clawed rake through the
    same acres,
gathering stacks, and dragged the wagon from stack to
    stack,
and the built hayrack back, up hill to the chaffy barn,
three loads of hay a day, hanging wide from the hayrack.

Sundays you trotted the two miles to church with the light
    load
of a leather quartertop buggy, and grazed in the sound of
    hymns.
Generation on generation, your neck rubbed the window
    sill
of the stall, smoothing the wood as the sea smooths glass.

When you were old and lame, when your shoulders hurt
    bending to graze,
one October the man who fed you and kept you, and
    harnessed you every morning,
led you through corn stubble to sandy ground above Eagle
    Pond,
and dug a hole beside you where you stood shuddering in
    your skin,

and lay the shotgun's muzzle in the boneless hollow behind
    your ear,
and fired the slug into your brain, and felled you into your
    grave,
shoveling sand to cover you, setting goldenrod upright
    above you,
where by next summer a dent in the ground made your
    monument.

For a hundred and fifty years, in the pasture of dead
    horses,
roots of pine trees pushed through the pale curves of your
    ribs,
yellow blossoms flourished above you in autumn, and in
    winter
frost heaved your bones in the ground—old toilers, soil
    makers:

O Roger, Mackerel, Riley, Ned, Nellie, Chester, Lady
    Ghost.

Dudley Fitts
TWO EPITAPHS

EPITAPH OF A MALTESE WATCH-DOG

Beneath me (says the stone) lies the white dog from Melita,
The faithful sentinel of Eumêlos' house:
                                        living,
His name was Bully Boy; but now, in death,
His barking is hushed in the empty ways of night.

—*Tymnes*

EPITAPH OF A PET HARE

Light-footed, floppy-eared,
The baby hare:
Snatched away from my mother to be the pet
Of sweet-skinned Phanion:
                              Spring blossoms
Were all my food,
                  my mother was soon forgotten:
But I died at last of surfeit of dewy petals!
Now beside her bed my mistress has made my grave,
Even in dreams to keep me close to her breast.

—*Meleagros*

(Translated by Dudley Fitts)

Marilyn Chin
WRITE, DO WRITE

And to you, the exiled one in Singkiang, waiting twenty
    years for the sun,
a large, hideous lantern strutting
over the barbarian wilderness—

wherever you are, don't forget me, please—
on heaven's stationery, with earth's chalk,
write, do write.

Valerie Linet

POETRY LOAVES

(serves those who are hungry)

Wash your hands. Rid them of a lifetime's hesitation.
Roll up your sleeves.
Keep paper towels on hand.
Preheat oven to 375°.
Combine flour and loud pauses for flavor.
Add spices to thrill away boredom:
cinnamon risk,
a dash of blanched candour to taste,
one-half teaspoon of doubt to balance.
Fill the room with baking smells.
Lose your hands in a mound of batter,
the hill of bound matter, not yet ready for climbing.
Knead the mixture until it tumbles into birth.
Cover dough with a damp cloth,
and rise to unseemly heights. The sun will appear
in this unbaked loaf.
Poem should double in bulk after one uncertain age
of introspection, many reincarnations, and editions.
Pound down dough; it will survive, and be the stronger for it.
Do not follow recipe too closely;
shut your eyes and burn the rules.
Roll into loaves of different shapes and sizes.
Even an outspoken lump has its place.

Denise Levertov
WRITING IN THE DARK

It's not difficult.
Anyway, it's necessary.

Wait till morning, and you'll forget.
And who knows if morning will come.

Fumble for the light, and you'll be
stark awake, but the vision
will be fading, slipping
out of reach.

You must have paper at hand,
a felt-tip pen—ballpoints don't always flow,
pencil points tend to break. There's nothing
     shameful in that much prudence: those are your tools.

Never mind about crossing your t's, dotting your i's—
but take care not to cover
one word with the next. Practice will reveal
how one hand instinctively comes to the aid of the other
to keep each line
clear of the next.

Keep writing in the dark:
a record of the night, or
words that pulled you from depths of unknowing,
words that flew through your mind, strange birds
crying their urgency with human voices,

or opened
as flowers of a tree that blooms
only once in a lifetime:

words that may have the power
to make the sun rise again.

Anonymous
DONAL OG

It is late last night the dog was speaking of you;
the snipe was speaking of you in her deep marsh.
It is you are the lonely bird through the woods;
and that you may be without a mate until you find me.

You promised me, and you said a lie to me,
that you would be before me where the sheep are flocked;
I gave a whistle and three hundred cries to you,
and I found nothing there but a bleating lamb.

You promised me a thing that was hard for you,
a ship of gold under a silver mast;
twelve towns with a market in all of them,
and a fine white court by the side of the sea.

You promised me a thing that is not possible,
that you would give me gloves of the skin of a fish;
that you would give me shoes of the skin of a bird;
and a suit of the dearest silk in Ireland.

When I go by myself to the Well of Loneliness,
I sit down and I go through my trouble;
when I see the world and do not see my boy,
he that has an amber shade in his hair.

It was on that Sunday I gave my love to you;
the Sunday that is last before Easter Sunday.
And myself on my knees reading the Passion;
and my two eyes giving love to you for ever.

My mother said to me not to be talking with you today,
or tomorrow, or on the Sunday;
it was a bad time she took for telling me that;
it was shutting the door after the house was robbed.

My heart is as black as the blackness of the sloe,
or as the black coal that is on the smith's forge;
or as the sole of a shoe left in white halls;
it was you put that darkness over my life.

You have taken the east from me; you have taken the west
     from me;
you have taken what is before me and what is behind me;
you have taken the moon, you have taken the sun from me;
and my fear is great that you have taken God from me!

(Translated by Lady Augusta Gregory)

William Carlos Williams
THE WINDS

flowing edge to edge
their clear edges meeting—
the winds of this northern March—
blow the bark from the trees
the soil from the field
the hair from the heads of
girls, the shirts from the backs
of the men, roofs from the
houses, the cross from the
church, clouds from the sky
the fur from the faces of
wild animals, crusts
from scabby eyes, scales from
the mind and husbands from wives

Judith Hemschemeyer
I REMEMBER THE ROOM
WAS FILLED WITH LIGHT

They were still young, younger than I am now.
I remember the room was filled with light
And moving air. I was watching him
Pick brass slivers from his hands as he did each night
After work. Bits of brass gleamed on his brow.
She was making supper. I stood on the rim
Of a wound just healing; so when he looked up
And asked me when we were going to eat
I ran to her, though she could hear. She smiled
And said 'Tell him . . .' Then 'Tell her . . .' On winged feet
I danced between them, forgiveness in my cup,
Wise messenger of the gods, their child.

Megan Gannon
SONG

In a cabin of ash-grey stone
resides a pair that's greyer still:
beside the hearth a man carves beasts,
a woman sews by the windowsill.

She stitches flax on coat lapels
and trims the sleeves with yellow gorse.
From elm he shapes a cock-eyed owl,
from evergreen, a three-legged horse.

The only food they need they pluck
From two plum trees and one pear tree,
for she's his bread and he's her wine
though she can't hear and he can't see.

e. e. cummings
"IF THERE ARE ANY HEAVENS
MY MOTHER WILL(ALL BY HERSELF)HAVE"

if there are any heavens my mother will(all by herself)have
one. It will not be a pansy heaven nor
a fragile heaven of lilies-of-the-valley but
it will be a heaven of blackred roses

my father will be(deep like a rose
tall like a rose)

standing near my

swaying over her
(silent)
with eyes which are really petals and see

nothing with the face of a poet really which
is a flower and not a face with
hands
which whisper
This is my beloved my

                    (suddenly in sunlight
he will bow,

& the whole garden will bow)

Robert Graves
A L L I E

Allie, call the birds in,
    The birds from the sky!
Allie calls, Allie sings,
    Down they all fly:
First there came
Two white doves,
    Then a sparrow from his nest,
Then a clucking bantam hen,
    Then a robin red-breast.

Allie, call the beasts in,
    The beasts, every one!
Allie calls, Allie sings,
    In they all run:
First there came
Two black lambs,
    Then a grunting Berkshire sow,
Then a dog without a tail,
    Then a red and white cow.

Allie, call the fish up,
The fish from the stream!
Allie calls, Allie sings,
Up they all swim:
First there came
Two gold fish,
A minnow and a miller's thumb,
Then a school of little trout,
Then the twisting eels come.

Allie, call the children,
Call them from the green!
Allie calls, Allie sings,
Soon they run in:
First there came
Tom and Madge,
Kate and I who'll not forget
How we played by the water's edge
Till the April sun set.

W. S. Merwin
DUSK IN WINTER

The sun sets in the cold without friends
Without reproaches after all it has done for us
It goes down believing in nothing
When it has gone I hear the stream running after it
It has brought its flute it is a long way

Jacob Nibenegenasabe
"ALL THE WARM NIGHTS"

All the warm nights
sleep in moonlight

keep letting it
go into you

do this
all your life

do this
you will shine outward
in old age

the moon will think
you are
the moon

(*Translated by Howard Norman*)

Theodore Roethke

FRAU BAUMAN, FRAU SCHMIDT, AND FRAU SCHWARTZE

Gone the three ancient ladies
Who creaked on the greenhouse ladders,
Reaching up white strings
To wind, to wind
The sweet-pea tendrils, the smilax,
Nasturtiums, the climbing
Roses, to straighten
Carnations, red
Chrysanthemums; the stiff
Stems, jointed like corn,
They tied and tucked,—
These nurses of nobody else.
Quicker than birds, they dipped
Up and sifted the dirt;
They sprinkled and shook;
They stood astride pipes,
Their skirts billowing out wide into tents,
Their hands twinkling with wet;
Like witches they flew along rows
Keeping creation at ease;
With a tendril for needle
They sewed up the air with a stem;
They teased out the seed that the cold kept asleep,—

All the coils, loops, and whorls.
They trellised the sun; they plotted for more than
themselves.

I remember how they picked me up, a spindly kid,
Pinching and poking my thin ribs
Till I lay in their laps, laughing,
Weak as a whiffet;
Now, when I'm alone and cold in my bed,
They still hover over me,
These ancient leathery crones,
With their bandannas stiffened with sweat,
And their thorn-bitten wrists,
And their snuff-laden breath blowing lightly over me
in my first sleep.

Mother Goose
"GO TO BED FIRST"

Go to bed first,
A golden purse;
Go to bed second,
A golden pheasant;
Go to bed third,
A golden bird.

Wallace Stevens
DISILLUSIONMENT OF TEN O'CLOCK

The houses are haunted
By white night-gowns.
None are green,
Or purple with green rings,
Or green with yellow rings
Or yellow with blue rings.
None of them are strange,
With socks of lace
And beaded ceintures.
People are not going
To dream of baboons and periwinkles.
Only, here and there, an old sailor,
Drunk and asleep in his boots,
Catches tigers
In red weather.

e. e. cummings
"ANYONE LIVED IN A PRETTY
HOW TOWN"

anyone lived in a pretty how town
(with up so floating many bells down)
spring summer autumn winter
he sang his didn't he danced his did.

Women and men(both little and small)
cared for anyone not at all
they sowed their isn't they reaped their same
sun moon stars rain

children guessed(but only a few
and down they forgot as up they grew
autumn winter spring summer)
that noone loved him more by more

when by now and tree by leaf
she laughed his joy she cried his grief
bird by snow and stir by still
anyone's any was all to her

someones married their everyones
laughed their cryings and did their dance
(sleep wake hope and then)they
said their nevers they slept their dream

stars rain sun moon
(and only the snow can begin to explain
how children are apt to forget to remember
with up so floating many bells down)

one day anyone died i guess
(and noone stooped to kiss his face)
busy folk buried them side by side
little by little and was by was

all by all and deep by deep
and more by more they dream their sleep
noone and anyone earth by april
wish by spirit and if by yes.

Women and men(both dong and ding)
summer autumn winter spring
reaped their sowing and went their came
sun moon stars rain

Eleanor Farjeon

JOSEPH FELL A-DREAMING

Joseph fell a-dreaming.
He dreamed of sheaves of grain;
One stood upright like a tree,
The rest bowed down again.

His dreams came with the night
And he told them in the noon.
He dreamed of the eleven stars,
The sun and the moon.

The sun was his father,
The moon was his mother,
Of all the stars, the brightest star
Was Benjamin his brother.

Philip Levine
MAKING LIGHT OF IT

I call out a secret name, the name
of the angel who guards my sleep,
and light grows in the east, a new light
like no other, as soft as the petals
of the blown rose of late summer.
Yes, it is late summer in the West.
Even the grasses climbing the Sierras
reach for the next outcropping of rock
with tough, burned fingers. The thistle
sheds its royal robes and quivers
awake in the hot winds off the sun.
A cloudless sky fills my room, the room
I was born in and where my father sleeps
his long dark sleep guarding the name
he shared with me. I can follow the day
to the black rags and corners it will
scatter to because someone always
goes ahead burning the little candle
of his breath, making light of it all.

Emily Dickinson
"WHO IS THE EAST?"

Who is the East?
The Yellow Man
Who may be Purple if He can
That carries in the Sun.

Who is the West?
The Purple Man
Who may be Yellow if He can
That lets Him out again.

NOTES ON THE POETS

ELIZABETH BISHOP *(1911–1979)* was born in Worcester, Massachusetts. She spent her first six years in Great Village, Nova Scotia, and lived for many years in Brazil. She was the consultant in poetry at the Library of Congress from 1949 to 1950. In 1956 she won the Pulitzer Prize for *Poems: North & South—A Cold Spring.*

WILLIAM BLAKE *(1757–1827)*, poet and artist, was born in London and worked all his life as an engraver. He is known to many young readers for his *Songs of Innocence* and *Songs of Experience,* which he printed by combining words and pictures on a single etched plate.

MICHAEL DENNIS BROWNE's most recent book is *Selected Poems 1965–1995.* He teaches at the University of Minnesota in Minneapolis.

MARILYN CHIN was born in Hong Kong and raised in Portland, Oregon. Her poetry books include *Dwarf Bamboo* and *The Phoenix Gone, the Terrace Empty.* She teaches creative writing at San Diego State University.

LUCILLE CLIFTON was born in Depew, New York, and began writing stories as a child. In addition to her collections of poems for adults, she has written many books for young people. Her honors include the Coretta Scott King Award. She is the mother of six children.

E. E. CUMMINGS *(1894–1962)*, poet, painter, and playwright, was born in Cambridge, Massachusetts. From age eight to twenty-two, he wrote a poem every day. During World War I he was an ambulance driver in France.

EMILY DICKINSON *(1830–1886)* lived all her life in Amherst, Massachusetts. In her later years, she grew increasingly reclusive. Only seven of the nearly two thousand poems found after her death were published during her lifetime.

"DONAL OG" is a traditional song, author unknown, which exists in many versions. It was translated from the Irish by the playwright and folklorist Lady Gregory (1852–1932), founder of the Irish National Theatre.

ELEANOR FARJEON *(1881–1965)* was born in South Hampstead, England, and was educated at home. She is best known for *Martin Pippin in the Apple Orchard, The Children's Bells: A Selection of Poems, The Glass Slipper,* and *The Little Bookroom,* which received the Hans Christian Andersen Award.

LIZ FISCHER grew up in Greensboro, North Carolina. She writes poems and makes movies.

DUDLEY FITTS *(1903–1968)*, poet and translator, was born in Boston. Two of his translations in this book, "Epitaph of a Maltese Watch-Dog" and "Epitaph of a Pet Hare," come from *Poems from the Greek Anthology,* a collection of more than four thousand poems written over a period of seventeen hundred years, starting in 700 B.C.

ROBERT FROST *(1874–1963)* was born in San Francisco, California, but lived most of his life in New England, which furnished the setting for many of his poems. He received many honors during his lifetime, including the Pulitzer Prize (four times) and the Congressional Gold Medal.

MEGAN GANNON was writing stories about magical birds and motherly kangaroos as soon as she could hold a pencil. She has lived in Tennessee, New York, Connecticut, New Hampshire, Massachusetts, and Ohio, and is an avid photographer with a strong interest in Swahili literature.

FEDERICO GARCÍA LORCA *(1898–1936)*, poet, playwright, and musician, was born in Fuentevaqueros, Granada, Spain. He was the artistic director of the state-sponsored traveling theatre group, University Theatre, known as La Barraca ("The Hut").

NIKKI GIOVANNI was born in Knoxville, Tennessee, and grew up in Cincinnati. In addition to her books for children and adults, she has made numerous sound recordings of her poetry. Her album, *Truth Is on Its Way* (1971), was the best-selling spoken-word album of the year. She has one son.

ROBERT GRAVES *(1895–1985)* is well known for his fiction and nonfiction books, and is the author of more than forty books of poetry. He was born in London and won the Queen's Gold Medal for Poetry in 1969. His books for children include *The Big Green Book,* illustrated by Maurice Sendak.

EMILY HAHN *(1905–1997)* was a freelance writer for the *New Yorker* who traveled extensively in China and Africa. She owned several apes and wrote about communication between humans and animals. *Eve and the Apes* and *China to Me: A Partial Autobiography* are two of her best-known books.

DONALD HALL was born in New Haven, Connecticut, and grew up in a house full of books, where his mother read poems aloud to him. He has read his poetry to audiences at more than a thousand community centers, schools, and universities. He edited *The Oxford Book of Children's Verse in America*. One of his books for children, *Ox-Cart Man*, won the Caldecott Medal.

JUDITH HEMSCHEMEYER has published three books of poetry: *I Remember the Room Was Filled With Light*, *Very Close and Very Slow*, and *The Ride Home*. She has also published a translation of Anna Akhmatova's poems.

GALWAY KINNELL, poet and translator, grew up in Rhode Island and began the serious study of poetry while he was a teenager at the Wilbraham Academy in Massachusetts. In 1983 his *Selected Poems* won the American Book Award and the Pulitzer Prize.

MAXINE KUMIN was born in Philadelphia, Pennsylvania, and in addition to her fiction and her books of poems, she has written nearly two dozen books for children. From 1981 till 1982, she was the poetry consultant to the Library of Congress. Her book of poems *Up Country: Poems of New England, New and Selected* won the Pulitzer Prize. She loves horses, and her deep knowledge of them has found its way into her poetry.

D. H. LAWRENCE *(1885–1930)*, the author of more than fifteen novels, collections of stories, and books of poems, was born in Eastwood, Nottinghamshire, England. His father was a coal miner and his mother was a schoolteacher. He wrote his first poems when he was nineteen.

DENISE LEVERTOV *(1923–1997)* was born in Ilford, England, and came to the United States at the age of twenty-five. Until she was thirteen, she and her sister were educated at home by their mother, who read aloud to them, both poetry and fiction. During World War II she served as a civilian nurse in London, and during the Vietnam War she was active in the antiwar movement. Her recent books include *Sands of the Well* and a collection of autobiographical essays, *Tesserae.*

PHILIP LEVINE grew up in Detroit, Michigan, during the Great Depression, and many of his poems have been shaped by his memories of this place. For many years he was a professor of English at California State University, Fresno. In 1995 he won the Pulitzer Prize for *The Simple Truth.*

RICHARD LEWIS's international anthologies of children's writing include *Miracles, Journeys, There Are Two Lives,* and *I Breathe a New Song.* He is the founder of the Touchstone Center for Children in New York, dedicated to innovative and nurturing approaches to teaching. "The Wind of the Marigold" was composed by a four-year-old Irish child, whose mother took down the words as Etain ran into her house, singing them.

VALERIE LINET has lived in Costa Rica and Honduras and Brooklyn. Writing poetry and baking bread are two of her passions.

W. S. MERWIN was born in New York City, the son of a Presbyterian minister. As a young child he wrote hymns for his father and illustrated them. He has translated extensively from French and Spanish. (His translation of García Lorca's "The Little Mute Boy" can be found in this anthology.) In 1971 he won the Pulitzer Prize for *The Carrier of Ladders.*

GABRIELA MISTRAL (Lucila Godoy Alcayaga) *(1889–1957),* poet, diplomat, and authority on rural education, was born in Vicuña, Chile, and began teaching primary school when she was fifteen. In 1945 she won the Nobel Prize for literature. Her book of children's poetry, *Tenura: Canciónes de niños* ("Tenderness: Songs of Children"), was published in 1924.

PABLO NERUDA *(1904–1973)* was born in a small farming community in southern Chile. Among his best-known works are *Residencia en la Tierra* ("Residence on Earth") and *Canto General* ("General Song"). The selection in this book is taken from *Odas Elementales* ("Elementary Odes"), a collection of poems that celebrate ordinary sights, sounds, animals, and objects. Neruda served as consul in Spain and in Mexico. In 1971, he was awarded the Nobel Prize for literature.

HOWARD NORMAN's interest in recording the rich legacy of storytelling in the Far North has taken him to arctic and subarctic Canada. His books include *Northern Tales: Traditional Stories of Eskimo and Indian Peoples, The Wishing Bone Cycle: Narrative Poems of the Swampy Cree Indians, Where the Chill Came From,* and *The Girl Who Dreamed Only Geese and Other Tales of the Far North.*

LINDA PASTAN grew up in New York City and graduated from Radcliffe College. Her recent collections of poems include *Heroes in Disguise, An Early Afterlife,* and *Carnival Evening.* A teacher for many years at the Bread Loaf Writers' Conference in Vermont, she is married and has three children.

KENNETH PATCHEN *(1911–1972),* born in Niles, Ohio, was both a poet and an artist who often included words in his paintings. He gave readings of his poetry to jazz accompaniment throughout the United States and Canada.

THEODORE ROETHKE *(1908–1963)* was born in Saginaw, Michigan, where his father and uncle owned a greenhouse business. A series of poems about the greenhouses appeared in his second book, *The Lost Son and Other Poems* (1948). He was twice awarded the National Book Award. *The Waking* won the Pulitzer Prize in 1954.

ALEXIS K. ROTELLA has written more than thirty books. The Jade Mountain Press published *Voice of the Mourning Dove* and *Looking for a Prince.* One of her specialties is haiku. She lives in Los Gatos, California.

CHRISTOPHER SMART *(1722–1771)* was born in Shipbourne, Kent, England, and worked as a writer for John Newbery, the publisher of children's books for whom the Newbery Medal is named. After a nervous breakdown, Smart was confined to an asylum, where he was allowed books, pen, ink, paper, and the company of his cat. During the four years he spent there, he wrote *Jubilate Agno,* the long poem from which "For I will consider my cat Jeoffry" is taken.

RADCLIFFE SQUIRES *(1917–1976)* was born in Salt Lake City, Utah, and taught for many years at the University of Michigan in Ann Arbor. His books include *Where the Compass Spins, Fingers of Hermes,* and *The Light under Islands.* He was an avid gardener.

WILLIAM SHAKESPEARE *(1564–1616),* playwright, poet, and actor, was born in Stratford-on-Avon and needs no introduction. The poem included in *Step Lightly* is from his last play, *The Tempest.*

WILLIAM STAFFORD *(1914–1993)* was born in Hutchinson, Kansas, and won the National Book Award in 1966 for *Traveling through the Dark.* He was a conscientious objector during World War II, and taught for thirty years at Lewis and Clark College in Oregon, with time away to serve as poetry consultant to the Library of Congress in 1970–71.

GERALD STERN has published nine books of poetry. He was born in Pittsburgh, Pennsylvania, and teaches writing at the University of Iowa in Iowa City. He has given poetry workshops and readings throughout the United States.

WALLACE STEVENS *(1879–1955)* was born in Reading, Pennsylvania. He was vice-president of the Hartford Accident and Indemnity Co. He won the National Book Award twice and won the Pulitzer Prize for *The Collected Poems of Wallace Stevens.*

KELLY WILLIAMS comes from Nashville, Tennessee. When she was in third grade, she wrote an award-winning song and sang it at the Country Music Hall of Fame. She is both a painter and a poet.

WILLIAM CARLOS WILLIAMS *(1883–1963)* was born in Rutherford, New Jersey, where he wrote poems, novels, and plays, and practiced medicine for forty years. Some of his poems were first written on prescription blanks. His *Pictures from Brueghel* won the Pulitzer Prize.

JAMES WRIGHT *(1927–1980)* was born in Martins Ferry, Ohio, and was the author of more than a dozen books of poetry. He has also published numerous translations. His *Collected Poems* won the Pulitzer Prize in 1972. The selection included in *Step Lightly* comes from his first book, *The Green Wall.*

WILLIAM BUTLER YEATS *(1865–1939)* was a poet and playwright who looked to Irish legends and songs for much of his material. He was born in Sandymount, Ireland, and was a cofounder of the Irish Literary Theatre and a senator of the Irish Free State. He won the Nobel Prize for Literature.

ACKNOWLEDGMENTS

For poem #101 ("Will there really be a 'Morning'?"): Poem #101 by Emily Dickinson from *The Complete Poems of Emily Dickinson*, edited by Thomas H. Johnson. Reprinted by permission of Little, Brown and Company.

For "For Caitlin Lally": © Michael Dennis Browne

For "The White Horse": "The White Horse" by D. H. Lawrence, from *The Complete Poems of D. H. Lawrence* by D. H. Lawrence, edited by V. de Sola Pinto & F. W. Roberts. Copyright © 1964, 1971 by Angelo Ravagli and C. M. Weekly, Executors of the Estate of Frieda Lawrence Ravagli. Used by permission of Viking Penguin, a division of Penguin Books USA, Inc.

For "Mutterings over the Crib of a Deaf Child": James Wright: "Mutterings over the Crib of a Deaf Child" from *Collected Poems*, © 1971 by James Wright, Wesleyan University Press by permission of University Press of New England.

For excerpt from "The Avenue Bearing the Initial of Christ into the New World": From "The Avenue Bearing the Initial of Christ into the New World," in *What a Kingdom It Was* by Galway Kinnell. Reprinted by permission of Houghton Mifflin Company. All rights reserved.

For "Turning the Tide" and "Cover Catfish": Liz Fischer: "Turning the Tide" and "Cover Catfish." Copyright 1998 by Liz Fischer.

For "The Wind of the Marigold": "The Wind of the Marigold" is by Etain Mary Clarke (age 5), from *Miracles: Poems by Children of the English-speaking World*. Edited by Richard Lewis. © 1966 by Richard Lewis. Presently distributed by the Touchstone Center for Children, Inc. New York, NY. Reprinted from *Parabola, The Magazine of Myth and Tradition*, Vol. VIII, No. 3 (summer, 1983).

For "Frau Bauman, Frau Schmidt, and Frau Schwartze," "Child on Top of a Greenhouse," and "Slug": "Frau Bauman, Frau Schmidt, and Frau Schwartze," copyright 1952 by Theodore Roethke. "Slug," copyright © 1955 by New Republic, Inc. "Child on Top of a Greenhouse," copyright 1946 by Editorial Publications, Inc., from *The Collected Poems of Theodore Roethke* by Theodore Roethke. Used by permission of Doubleday, a division of Bantam Doubleday Dell Publishing Group, Inc.

For "Come into Animal Presence": By Denise Levertov, from *Poems 1960–1967*. Copyright © 1966 by Denise Levertov. Reprinted by permission of New Directions Publishing Corp.

For "Cow Worship": "Cow Worship" by Gerald Stern was first published in *The Red Coal*.

For "The Little Mute Boy": By Federico García Lorca, translated by W. S. Merwin, from *The Selected Poems of Federico García Lorca*. Copyright © 1955 by New Directions Publishing Corp. Reprinted by permission of New Directions Publishing Corp.

For "Credo": "Credo" from *Looking for Luck* by Maxine Kumin. Copyright © 1992 by Maxine Kumin. Reprinted by permission of W. W. Norton & Company, Inc.

For "The Song of Wandering Aengus": Reprinted with the permission of Simon & Schuster from *The Collected Works of W. B. Yeats, Volume 1: The Poems*. Revised and edited by Richard J. Finneran (New York: Macmillan, 1989).

For "La Manca" (The Little Girl that Lost a Finger): By Gabriela Mistral, translated by Muna Lee, from *Anthology of Contemporary Latin-American Poetry*, edited by Dudley Fitts. Copyright © 1947 by Dudley Fitts. Reprinted by permission of New Directions Publishing Corp.

For "The Witch of Coös": From *The Poetry of Robert Frost*, edited by Edward Connery Lathem. Copyright 1951 by Robert Frost, copyright 1923, © 1969 by Henry Holt & Co., Inc. Reprinted by permission of Henry Holt & Co., Inc.